THE SANITY PATROL HANDBOOK

Z. SHARON GLANTZ

THE SANITY PATROL PRESS

thesanitypatrol.com   Seattle, Washington

The Sanity Patrol Press
937 North 90th Street
Seattle, WA 98103
thesanitypatrol.com

ISBN 0-9740775-0-X

Printed in the United States by Morris Publishing
3212 East Highway 30
Kearney, NE 68847
1-800-650-7888

Thanks Mom (aka Mary Ann Danin)
Elaine Gowell and Char
Patrollers Extraordinaire

TABLE OF CONTENTS

III. Anti-Patroller Management

THE SANITY PATROL IS OUT TO GET YOU

The Sanity Patrol is out to get you
You, the uncategorical, scavenging the mundane for meaning
You, the seeker, expanding understanding until it bursts into cathartic insight
You, the unique, conjuring new perspectives by unloading old baggage
You, the choreographer, gracefully entwining artistry with authenticity
Yes
The Sanity Patrol has come
How do you greet them?
Relief and fear
I'm okay? you exclaim
The Sanity Patrol refuses to pass judgment on your
enigmatic idiosyncratic virtuousity
No
You are not alone
On the contrary
You're part of a greater whole
The Sanity Patrol knows how to
      dance with circumstance
      embrace disgrace
      release the beast
Laughter is what they're after
The world's a giant cookie jar
Will you chip in?

I. MEMBERSHIP CRITERIA

YOU MAY ALREADY BE A MEMBER

Do you qualify for the Sanity Patrol?
Exactly how sane are you?

If when answering as to the status of your sanity
you exclude absolutes
you could still be sane
because black and white are not primary colors

Even if you're crazy, nuts, bonkers, loony tunes
you could still be sane
because you manage your madness
at least most of the time

Even if you go through periods of irrationality, rage, ridiculousness
you could still be sane
because you clean up any messes you may have made
After blurting out badly
you re-express the core feelings appropriately
Sanity Patrollers do this so no residue of stinky yuck remains
that is often odiferous and offensive to others
You may not be able to smell it yourself
or if you do you may like the stench
because it is familiar

SANITY NECESSITIES

Patrollers create their own criteria as they go along
but recognize certain necessities that assert sanity:

1 – DENIAL SUCKS
Denial creates an internalized feud
until the repressed puke is spewed
leaving you vulnerable in the nude
humiliated by being you

2 – GET OVER RESISTANCE
Remove the pole from your pants
that limits the fluidity of the dance
You can release through raves and rants
the inspiration to take a chance

3 – NO LIE FLIES
It's not easy to keep track
of to whom you said what and back
The pressure is bound to make a crack
between the fiction and the fact

4 – STOP DOING THAT

Again and again repeating an action
each time receiving no satisfaction
indicates sanity is off a fraction
resulting in membership retraction

5 – SO YOU FEEL SOMETHING

You do not live on this planet alone
and no one who lives is made of stone
which means emotions shade the tone
of all that is and will be known

6 – EXPRESS YOUR MESS

Your feelings are going to show anyway
like opinions they demand to have their say
Thinking is but one way
you make it through each and every day

7 – CAUSE AND EFFECT HAPPEN

If an action is intentionally taken
consequences cannot be forsaken
You may find you have a stake in
how intentions are easily mistaken

THE SANITY PATROL HANDBOOK

8 – OBTAIN COMMON SENSE, PLEASE
Though not as common as should be
logic and reason are priority
when dealing patiently with the immensity
of the ever-evolving human density

NOTHING MORE THAN FEELINGS

Patrollers know that to be 100% sane 100% of the time is madness
indicating a severe lack of imagination and individuation
There is a fine line between
emotional agitation and inspiration
Feelings can be managed
but they cannot be perfectly controlled
No
Perfection is an orientation, not a place
so don't bother trying to go there

Would that sanity meant all emotion simply disappeared
although isn't that what robots are for?
Too bad
So sad
Feeling is endemic to living
So pick a simile and smile:

Feelings are like driftwood
     they float until they beach
     where they are bleached and smoothed
     by the comings and goings of the tide

THE SANITY PATROL HANDBOOK

Feelings are like visits from Aunt Selma
    who shows up one day seeking refuge
    stays and overstays until
    she finally moves back to the flow of her own life

Feelings are like eating beans
    that fill your stomach with satisfaction
    Extra air builds pressure to escape your bloated gut
    until flatulence offers escape and relief

Feelings are reminders that
    it's okay to saturate someone else's shoulder
    with tears of snot and grief
    until their warmth dehydrates the wet

Like the Chinese proverb says,
    A pound of knowledge requires
    ten pounds of common sense
    to convert it into wisdom

Yes, Patrollers, you can be disturbed
as long as it doesn't disrupt your desire to remain sane
or the need to embrace the consensus reality shared with others
who you may or may not like
even when they are fellow Patrollers

THE SANITY PATROL HANDBOOK

II. GOALS OF THE SANITY PATROL

SIGMOS

The Sanity Patrol doesn't bother to ask:
What is the meaning of life?
Why?
Because the answer is in the question
Meaning? you ask
Meaning, yes, meaning is the answer
and meaning is the Sanity Patrol's primary goal
The meaning of what? you ask
Not the meaning of
No
Consider the meaning from
      meaning from love
      meaning from success
      meaning from satisfaction
      meaning from sigmos

Sigmos?
What the hell's a sigmo?
A sigmo is a significant moment
and significant moments are the basis of meaning

However
without a backstory
what could be a sigmo

is merely a moment
that may or may not maintain long term attention
Sigmos culminate less significant moments
and require a great deal of hard work

Consider these seven sigmo scenarios:

1. LOVE

You finally invited him out for coffee
He shrugged when he accepted
He had no idea your crush on him was so intense
It took all the courage you could muster
to ask him out
This is a sigmo unto itself
but an even more powerful sigmo
when part of the backstory

So here you are and here he is
Coffee stimulates your already vibrant conversation
You've proved yourselves compatible
as you comfortably share verbiage
while showing lots of teeth
Coffee helps set free the barriers
holding back the hormonal dance
adding sexual tension to the mix

Your exchanges reinforce your foolish grins
letting laughter periodically explode
even if inappropriate and completely off topic

He walks you to your car
gently knocking your shoulder
in a syncopated rhythm
that is like music for your soul
As you unlock the door
he turns your body towards him
looks deeply into your eyes
as he strokes the side of your face
His eyes briefly glance at your lips
He leans in and feathers them with his own
only to return gently and more firmly
pressing his face against yours
A lightening bolt shoots your gut
and you silently groan with pleasure
He leans back to look deeply into your eyes
his dumb grin reflecting your own
assuring you he will call you later
before dashing off quickly
leaving you standing there with keys dangling
watching his receding figure
your hand absently touching your lips

THE SANITY PATROL HANDBOOK

For the rest of the day
and at least a few to follow
you replay this sigmo over and over again
reigniting the fire in your belly
and other delicious reactions

2. GRIEF

He was a cat
and not a particularly nice one at that
You still hear him cleaning himself
right by your ear
as you struggle to fall asleep
That sandpaper sound
grating your comfort zone
was the white noise that sent you
resting with the Sandman
No matter how many times
you kicked him off the bed
he would return
to scrape the day off his fur
You knew he was old
He could die any time
yet you couldn't imagine him gone

You had trouble with his presence
loving and hating his self-containment
frustrated that he was not very affectionate
only purring when weaving through your legs
usually because he wanted to food or catnip

His death wasn't particularly remarkable
yet waves of sadness permeate your being
accompanied by periodic moments of rage
with guilt-ridden dashes of relief
You have no explanation
for the depth of your grief
until
until
until you remember your father's funeral
That was 30 years ago
All you really remember of him
was his habit of tapping his fingers
No matter where he was or what you were doing
his tapping served as background
a rhythm like your cat's licks
a similar annoyance you learned to accept
as part of who he was
You were 12 when Daddy died
You hardly cried for him because
you didn't know how to cry

Page 17

Now you cry with wracking sobs
old grief ignited by new grief
It hurts so so deep
yet it feels so real
and makes everything else more genuine

3. TRANSCENDANCE

You're an actor and you act
although mostly you react
You seek to get in sync with the ensemble
as together you move the action forward
finding the wave and riding it
kind of like emotional surfing
A writer has created the opportunity
for cresting the wave
so the audience gets sucked right in
But acting is not a matter of pretending
It has more to do with being
and being someone else is not as easy as it seems

During the process of rehearsal
hopefully without an audience
there is a special moment
when you cross the line
The line is between you and your character

Crossing it resembles being pummeled
by the crashing surf
completely out of control
Up is down, down is up
You are you, you are them
What is inside emerges outward
The emotional rush lets you know
you have merged with the character
as you break down and let tears
liquify the boundaries between you
In future work on the piece
you will know from whence you speak
because you know exactly where
the character lives within you
Every actor thrills at this moment
It resembles transcendence
on the crest of that very special wave

4. VISION

You're writing a novel
a feat unto itself
You've outlined and refined
the flow the text should take
You've thought through your characters
and know what motivates

But something is missing
You worry you procrastinate
rather than writing like a writer should
since a writer is a writer only when having written
So maybe you're only dreaming
and your novel is a figment of imagination
It's a figment with no pigment
to give it substance and dimension

Until one day
you're brushing your teeth
the way you do daily
It's an action requiring no thought
an autonomic action
As you spit the second time
the missing piece manifests
the main character's other flaw
that he must overcome which means...

Your vision of the story
shifts into a new reality
You can feel the pen calling you
You can hardly wait to respond
The actual writing of the work
feels more like a transcription
and the flow is too easy to be real

THE SANITY PATROL HANDBOOK

You remember that creativity
is not always linear
It comes in spurts and pops
bringing cohesiveness to seeming chaos
A creative work reaching completion
is the result of extensive processing
sometimes fearfully nonsensical
requiring faith and tenacity

Sigmos are found throughout the process
which is why wannabes and dabblers
only taste the delicious possibilities
But if a meal is what is wanted
the just desserts of completion are divine
adding the requisite backstory
to a sigmo extraordinaire

5. SYNCHRONICITY

Have you ever found religion
while pumping gas?
or maybe spiritual enlightenment
changing your underpants?
If you haven't, not to worry
You are not alone

For most Patrollers it takes more
than seeing Jesus in a dirty window
Passive observance isn't enough
to turn an observance into a sigmo

Sometimes you must work harder
to find dots to connect
until that moment when
the dots connect themselves
Say you have to make a decision between
two paths you might take:

One leads you towards helping individuals
working therapeutically one on one
helping one person at a time
find a healthier future to divine
You use your own brand of technique
to help remove the blocks that wreak
havoc on their ability to seek
the source of what prevents them
from being just fine

But you could also take the path
that leads more toward community
working in the trenches
and doing your duty

THE SANITY PATROL HANDBOOK

to help those in terrible need
with no lives except to breed
creating more mouths than they can feed
these are folks who could benefit
from a little charity

Your heart swells at the possible futures
and your gut clenches because
the decision is now
yet you haven't a clue of what to do

You stop for some ice cream
to soothe your trials and tribulations
You notice a woman stealing a ham
hiding it deep inside her coat
She sees you see her
and from her eye falls a tear
She returns the ham to the display
and humbly walks away
You remember that Easter
when your family had ham
because someone had given your mother
a helping hand
She had exchanged cleaning for meat
and provided you with a feast

THE SANITY PATROL HANDBOOK

You finish your shopping
your brain no longer hopping
your decision has been made
thanks to the synchronicity
of a potential shoplifter

On your way out the door
you see the woman wiping the nose
of a cranky two year old
while the older child stares out into space
You give the woman a ham
wink your eye, squeeze her hand
and continue at your usual pace
on the path you know you'll take

Some Patrollers choose to believe in coincidence
Others embrace the sigmos of synchronicity
All it requires is paying attention
to the details that surround you
and making significant connections

6. FORTUNE-TELLING

Creative obsessive-compulsive actions
are not always unhealthy
and provide insight or even oracles
Your morning routine includes various actions
where timing could condition your day
You have two major signals to drive through
before hitting the highway

    If you make the tail end of one
        the second requires only a short wait
    If you have to wait at the first
        you'll be waiting at the second
    If your timing is just right
        you'll drive through both without stopping

When you get to the parking lot
ease of parking is variable
depending on the activities in the building

    Sometimes it's too packed to park and you drive to another lot
    Sometimes the traffic in the lot makes parking difficult
    Sometimes there are spaces galore and you park in front of the front door

THE SANITY PATROL HANDBOOK

The elevators are slow
and have minds of their own
with priorities unknown

     Maybe it takes five minutes of waiting for a car
          and fellow passengers are cranky
     Maybe the wait is short with a talkative crowd
          but the chat is exclusive and dull
     Maybe a car arrives promptly with a crowd
          of like-minded smart asses who make you laugh out loud

Imagine a day, just any old day when you
     hit the signals timely
     flow easily through traffic
     find the perfect spot to park
     enter the elevator immediately
     and chat with the sassy girl of your dreams

This is a series of sigmos to say the least
culminating in a greater sigmo because of the cumulative feats
All right, so it's not major or deeply philosophical
but sigmos can be like that
with minimal meaning from the backstory
yet a sigmo all the same

7. PERFORMANCE

Not all Patrollers were meant to grace the stage
and share the magic that is they
Some like the background
being one in the masses
not standing up or sticking out
or gaining special attention
Yet desires and reality do not always mesh
and the need for performance can be impressed

You're driving and find yourself in a busy intersection
You have to make a left turn yet the traffic is wild
The signal doesn't have an arrow
forcing you to find your own moment
to continue along your way
There are cars behind you
impatiently awaiting your next move
The light turns green
You pull out into the middle of the intersection
as cars rush past you both ways
putting tremors into your chassie
The light turns yellow
the last fellow passes on your left
and now is the moment
for your performance

Will you pop the clutch and stall?
Will you turn awkwardly or crawl?
Maybe you'll take too long
and hear honking from the throng
All eyes await your turn
so they can move forward on their way
But the pressure doesn't cause dismay
as you turn left and in your new lane stay
A sigmo albeit a lesser sigmo
can occur with a simple left turn
A more intense sigmo would occur if
          a car ran the light or
          a major accident occurred

Patrollers know that not all sigmos are good
but they are meaningful nonetheless
putting color into the gray of regularity
There is no one meaning to life
There are many roads to hoe
from the daily significant moments
to the great satisfaction of a passing sigmo

III. ANTI-PATROLLER MANAGEMENT

UNCONVENTION OUTSIDE THE CONVENTION

The Sanity Patrol periodically holds a convention
for continuing education and training new recruits
Have you received your invitation?

Nonmembers of the Sanity Patrol
are known as anti-patrollers
Some anti-patrollers biochemically refuse sanity
More anti-patrollers embrace membership criteria
of their own dubious design
The Sanity Patrol is not about rigid rules but
recognizes an anti-patroller when they see one
at least most of the time

Conventions are an opportunity to see
collectives of anti-patrollers in action
so they can be better
  identified
  catagorized
  and dealt with accordingly
Only one anti-patroller collective is selcted
to perform at a Sanity Patrol convention
although many others try to attend

THE SANITY PATROL HANDBOOK

The Curmudgeon Collective

is on strike outside the event
"What for?" they cry, "Sanity perpetuates insanity
the ratio of sane to insane will always remain consistent
and generally humanity sucks"

The Altruist's Organization

put their rose-colored glasses
back on the bridges of their noses
paste smug grins on their faces
and shuffle back and forth past the happening
demonstrating their active apathy

The Ernest Seekers

come without invitation
and try to baaaaa their way in
and block the entrance with their flock

The Psychobabble Self-Helpers

meet outside the convention
believing themselves to be inside
They alter their attitudes, verbalize and reverbalize
sharing their outer most feelings
They empathize and sympathize
convincing themselves they've done more than scratch the surface
which they haven't because they can't

The Spiritual Evangelists
set up a tent outside the convention
where they replace sanity with insanity
and call it transcendence

The Realism Junkies
try to set up road blocks
through acts of Darwinism and detente
"Say no to everything except what is," they smirk
unaware of their pending death due to a lack of imagination
and the inability to think in the abstract

Each **Narcissist** represents their own organization
although they are easily distracted
by their images reflected off of any shiny surface

Fill-in-the-Blank Anonymous Members
hand out coffee
in between claiming responsibility
and submitting to God

The Fundamentalists
try to convert the **Anonymous** members
and any one else they can
by smashing their heads with bibles
in the name of Jehovah, Jesus, Allah or Bob

The Borderline Personality Disorders join **The Perpetrators of Abuse**
dramatically depart the demonstration
to indulge in symbiotic anti-patroller behaviors
they mistake for love and affection

The Depressed
hold a sit-in and sit quietly
except for the **Bi-Polars**
who periodically vibrate with such intensity they take flight

Uninvited Psychiatrists
hand out colorful tablets of drugs and placebos
in exchange for greenbacks and awards

Psychologists Without Invitations
try to calm demonstrators
before succumbing and joining in

One collective calls themselves **Artists of Sanity**
They dress without taste or distaste
claiming their obnoxiousness is a creative compulsion

In every collective outside the convention
volumes of **Victims** pretend to commit suicide
or make whining sounds they mistake for music

The only group the Sanity Patrol lets in
for entertainment purposes only
are the **Psychic Vampires**
They are the ungrateful dead seeking redemption
in a rite of their own design
The Sanity Patrol is fascinated
as they perform their rite:

> "Rise from your graves for the reckoning
> Grope through the filth that has buried you
> Worm through layers of sediment and sentiment
> We are what we were yet we are not what we once were
> Our eyes are of tempered glass
> protecting what is within from what is without
>
> Our pallor is suffocated gray
> Our hair and nails frozen since death
> except for those few more inches
> that grew after
>
> We are embalmed
> preserving our memory of life
> We crave release from this state and seek Final Judgment
> Curse us and we will be free me free me free me"

Patrollers giggle because they know
freedom is the last thing they really want
They would much rather remain encased in their lifeless bodies
to pine about what once was
while sucking the life out of others

> "We welcome the ultimate cruel authority
> who criticizes, patronizes
> and ostracizes our being and nonbeing
> Yes, we are wretched
> and yes, our bodies and minds have renounced
> growth, change or transformation
> Yet this is what we crave"

They beat their breasts
with the long suffering cries of an infant who will remain an infant
Once the rite of self-pity is completed
the Psychic Vampires try to do the room
by sucking away whatever essence remains
But they cannot succeed
Not at this convention
Here they can only suck empty air
They are thanked
> paid with love – not blood
> and ushered out
"Maybe next year," the staff says to the crowds outside the door

THE VICARIOUS DUMPING GROUNDS

Every now and then
a Patroller is challenged
by provocative anti-patrollers
Awareness remains clear but the internal workings spoil
and begin to resemble some ancient once-living occupant
of an unused refrigerator

Uh oh

Issues of dysfunction threaten the Patroller's ability to maintain membership
Human frailty invites the Patroller to disengage
and join with the egoless ethicless awkward anti-patrollers that provoke them
Anti-patrollers thrive on entropy or chaos
a staple in their diet that keeps them just together enough to function

Nothing to be done
It can't be fixed

But even if the Patroller rejects these paradigms, what of catharsis?
Situations have no space within themselves for resolution

Uh oh

A decision must be made

No
the Patroller is not corrupt, merely momentarily irrational
However
The toxic residue of interaction with anti-patrollers
starts oozing into the poores of the Patrollers
requiring an appropriate outlet

The Patroller searches until it finds the Vicarious Dumping Grounds
before the residue seeps into the cracks and rots the carefully constructed fabric
keeping the membership card bonded
The Vicarious Dumping Grounds are a faraway land within arms' length
aching to be fed the scum and slime emitted during human relativity
and in rare circumstance
cosmic relatively disguised as humanness
The search is laborious
The pathway is full of traps

THE TRAP OF COMPROMISE
Unmindful compromise helps the waste expand and grow
The awareness of the Sanity Patrol becomes
    blocked and congested
    clogged with more and more gunk
The willingness to make sacrifices is only a pretense
and means of avoiding conflict taken personally
During endless senseless negotiations
the trapped waste exponentially toxifies

THE TRAP OF FORGETFULNESS

Forgetfulness breeds karma of the undesirable sort
Where active inaction may be required
this trap lets inactive action
serve as a blindfold
allowing toxicity to exist
by pretending it isn't even there
or worse – assuming it can't possibly exist
and therefore it won't exist
Contractions of different ways of being
become more important than the subject toxicity
The result is a chain reaction of forgetfulness

THE TRAP OF IMPOSED IGNORANCE

Flinging about ignorance acts as a boomerang
The waste dons an infinite variety of disguises
instilling patterns of a deniable nature
Circumstances remain in the mundane
with no ramifications of anything larger
"I don't know" is not an answer
it's only a diversion
No
Ignorance is not bliss
merely a way to avoid resolution
and toxic waste disposal

THE TRAP OF FORGIVENESS
Empty forgiveness puts clumsiness into the grace of a Patroller
if that forgiveness is like a fig rotting from the inside out
The surface appearance of forgiveness
 can be worse than deceiving
it can be deadly
Forgiveness takes more than the removal of fig leaves
to share in an intimate vision or a vision of intimacy

THE TRAP OF PRIDE
Patrollers who parade pride put themselves
in the arena with the gladiators of insanity
a troop far more dangerous than the anti-patrollers
because games become real
If losing, the power of the Patroller is depleted
leaving an illusion of endurance
as sturdy as the worn out pants of a young growing boy
The power of the Patroller's pride eventually corrupts
when the threads of sanity are pulled too hard
and the weave so carefully entwined unravels

With tenacity and humor a Patroller can move past the traps
along the path to the Vicarious Dumping Grounds

The Vicarious Dumping Grounds
        absorbs all toxins
        embraces all garbage
        and invites all trash to a baseball game
With post-constipated relief
the toxic waste emitted during human relativity finds a home

What a relief
You are now renewed, refreshed and ready for more

THE SANITY PATROL HANDBOOK

SIN CAN CREATE SANITY INSECURITY

The Sanity Patrol doesn't necessarily believe in sin
However
some Patrollers do and besides
sin is a terrific metaphor
Patrollers from differing areas of expertise and culture
have divergent spins on sin
and how to avoid judgments and black/white arguments
Sin isn't so much the product of evil
but that inappropriate ick
too crusted over to package
and take to the Vicarious Dumping Grounds

leaving a revolting residue
that can only wear off in time
because no cleaner is capable
of removing it any other way

THE PHYICIST PATROLLER SAYS:
Sin is the relationship between
a black hole and a white hole
They constantly seduce and reject one another
and in their embraces they fabricate reality
Sometimes they use quantum foam
the ultimate universal contraceptive

THE SANITY PATROL HANDBOOK

although it's failure is why we're here
Thus we are relatively safe using the old in and out model
in and out, in and out
We avoid voids
They are the dark sins
of sociopaths and child molesters

Consider the jelly doughnut
Careful
Jelly alone cannot prevent unwanted incarnations
The jelly in our doughnut is singularity
and what is singularity?
the core of the black hole
Castration, premature ejaculation and oozing infection live there
To connect with singularity is to become
an insatiable nymphomaniac who is
      HIV-positive
      with Hepatitis C
      syphilis
      herpes
      and genital warts
Scared of singularity? Good

Now what of the dough?
Let's assume our doughnut was not fried long enough

and some of the dough is mushy and gummy
This gummy zone is kind of kinky
All your strangest and most bizarre fantasies live there
You know the ones so don't deny it
Yes you do know so knock it off
and imagine the lifestyle

If you really wanted to leave the gummy zone
the Penrose Mechanism might help
bouncing you through the gumminess to the crispier dough
The crispy dough is healthy dough
because it is kneaded by the Sanity Patrol
and fried in imagination and metaphor

However
after an adventure into the gummy zone
you observe a new normalness and reality alterations
All is similar yet out of sync with memory's rhythm
Careful, that rhythm method of relativity is risky as well
Sin isn't so bad if you are in and out
Avoid voids
and don't spend a lot of time
in gummy zones

THE PSYCHOLOGIST PATROLLER SAYS:
Sin is passivity
The avoidance of direct dealing through distraction or denial
this is the source of sin
Discounting helps disguise the core feeling layer by layer
until agitation and escalation ingratiate your comfort zone
The unease creates dis-ease
infecting your health and personal welfare

For example
take the core feeling of fear
I'm frightened
I'm scared

First layer, conceptualize the fear
        I fear the unknown
        Incomprehensibility is terrifying
        I want to know everything so that
        nothing unknown sneaks up and bites my butt

Second layer, distract to what is known
        I know a hell of a lot of important stuff
        yet I'm open to learning more
        because that which I don't know
        someone else out there will know

Third layer, deny the fear
        What could I possibly be afraid of?
        I'm safe, secure and protected
        I'm just being silly
        I will rise above it
        and put a stop to all of this nonsense

Fourth layer, discount the existence of the unknown
        If I needed to know anything more
        I'd have already learned it by now
        I know all I need to know
        End of story

Layer upon layer protects the defenses
Layer upon layer defends the protections
The core of fear is unsafely, insecurely obscured
like a tumor, it is discomforting, causing unease, inflicting disease
The symptoms?
Seemingly irrational reactions
        The sky is perfectly clear, damn it
        so quit pretending I'm acting superior
Emotions get hooked by unlikely bait
        How dare you tell me I'm being irrational
        I'm fine, damn it, perfectly fine

Inappropriate zaps are fun and powerful at one moment
only to become humiliating and guilt-ridden in the next
  Your manliness is as miniscule as your ability to communicate
  and this pretense that I'm superior really sucks
  Then again, I only yell at those I truly love
  So I must love you a lot
The fear of fear overwhelms through self-destructive violence
sometimes manifested outside the self
but more likely a cultivated cancer from within
  How could I say such terrible things
  I must be a bad bad person
The core seeks out stronger and more grandiose distractions
  Some day I'll be as clear as the sky
  and everyone will know it
  especially you
  and then you will love me forever
The core creates more dramatic denials
  It's not you, it's me
  even though I'm right as rain
  so hate me if you must
  or we can talk about the weather
The discounts depress and compress the layers around the core
creating more and more pressure
  I'll be fine, really – really really fine
  I will be, you'll see

THE SANITY PATROL HANDBOOK

The pressure increases
       Everything is fine – really really fine
       Can't you tell how fine it is?
       Can't you? Can't you? Can't you?
Distract from denials
Deny discounts
Discount distractions
The fear of fear of fear agitates, exponentiates and escalates until

BOOM

Sadly, the disease is not cured, merely momentarily disseminated
drumming up more dramas to follow
Sure, the pressure is released for the moment
but the core will seek out more protections
and cycle through the same old same old
again and again and again

BOOM

This is the birth of sin

THE SOCIOLOGIST PATROLLER SAYS:

What the hell is going on? You call this civilized?
Look around you
Better yet, take a deep breath and try not to cough
I dare you
We're pooping in the air and the air embraces the scumful molecules
      as though they belonged together
      as though they were soul mates
The air is adapting like all the wildlife
to our thorough infestation of the planet
Wildlife adapts by becoming extinct because they no longer have a habitat
Sinful

American imperialism in the guise of McDonalds makes for a world of Big Macs
Do you know what's in a Big Mac?
Do you really really know hmmm?
You are what you eat, Mac
Sinful

How about a limited nuclear war?
as if there such a thing were possible
To prepare, how about a practice nuclear war?
The bell dings and we pretend we're radioactive survivors
So what if it's a little gross
We mutate or die

THE SANITY PATROL HANDBOOK

It's new age consciousness raising
or maybe it's corporate training
Sinful

Rules, rules and more rules
Can you keep track?
Careful, taboo will make voodoo of what you do.
Don't – uh uh – bad – no
Behave or be punished
Be good or be banished
Value or be devaluated
Make love not libel or you'll be in court not courtship
Vote or have your choices surgically removed with such precision
you'll never know you had them
Sinful

Communicate via email or chat
Make brief cell phone calls
You can talk intimately without sharing anything personal
And if the messages are intercepted so what
you will remain safe and protected
because no one really listens anyway
unless said in the size and shape of a sound bite
Watch the news and learn about the world
via hyperbole and onomatopoeia
created for those with the attention span of a gnat
Sinful

The rich get richer, the poor get poorer
and the middle class is thrust
upwards or downward
thanks to creative corporate accounting
deregulation, regional delegation and downright greed
Sometimes strategies are sponsored by government
who we pay to protect us
although lately less from one another
and more from those evil terrorists
a useful and mutable term
dependent upon the war du jour
Sinful

And despite the horrors of the holocaust
mass genocide among the masses amasses
for those seeking to assert some kind of mythical superiority
rather than working together for a better life
because blame is a game
of pissing and hissing
and my stink's skankier than yours
Diversity is cool as long as no one has to change
or reach outside their comfort zone
and get to know one of ... ahem ... them
Sinful

Adultery is for those tired of being adults
Guard your guardians
Glorify your gurus
Answer to your authorities
Leave it to them
They know what's best
They'll take care of you
Obey them or forever hold your opinions

So what the hell is going on?
Did I do something wrong?
That is impossible because I am me
Yes, I'm okay, but you...

A LAWYER PATROLLER SAYS:
Comes now the petitioner herein
by and through their attorney
and moves the court to strike
the very notion that sin exists
This motion is based on
personal knowledge and belief
and the many declarations made by
religious writers who often make
adjoining yet contradictory claims

THE SANITY PATROL HANDBOOK

using their own verbiage and dogma
drawing upon their own pantheon
of a spiritually sacred entity or entities
Because all scenarios of sin
contain mitigating factors
each scenario demands its own personal trial
which may have to include more than
two opposing parties
whose complex relationships
our system of advesarial justice
may not be able to accommodate
Justice is not blind
she is merely blindfolded
seeking the balance of dualization
so that society feels safer and more in control
over those who have gone astray

The court does not have the necessary jurisdiction
to pass judgment over the greater entity or entities
the religious specialists depict
If the court had this sort of jurisdiction
those in the judicial system would have to assume
that they are God

THE SANITY PATROL HANDBOOK

THE SANITY PATROL HANDBOOK

Despite press to the contrary
most officers of the court
do not want to play God
because responsibility without authority or power
leaves a lot to be desired
Those who do not reap the karma
of trying to play God
learn to make a friend of humiliation
in both the court and in their personal lives
Holding the life of a person or persons
in a pleading or brief
begs for careful responsibility without omniscience
rather than pretentious pomposity
Thus the need for court rules and procedures
designed by those who use the system
often for better or worse
helps balance resolution and justice

Blame is a legal strategy
that encourages the articulation of evil or sin
But it is really a tragedy that oversimplifies
the complexities of an individual's life
and can easily be dismissed
within a greater context

Within the justice system itself
      there is no good or bad
      there is no right or wrong
      there are no absolutes
      even if the outcomes appeal to our desire of such
That's not to say the system
is always fair and just
You get as much justice
as you can afford
But despite the periodic unfairness
poverty is not a sin
It's just one more mitigating factor
proving sin is not absolute
but a mutable mass
of personal morality
based on personal knowledge and beliefs

THE WITCH PATROLLER SAYS:
There is no black magick or white magick
There is only magick
If you want it to be a sin
to practice the magickal arts
that is your choice

THE SANITY PATROL HANDBOOK

Most major religions include
a magickal sect or
accommodate those who push
the limits of doctrine

If you are a Catholic
you could perform a magickal act
that might be considered a sin
confess it to your priest
do whatever he says
and then go about your business
which may include additional sinning

If you are a Jew
you could become a Cabalist
who focuses on words, letters and sounds
when seeking the meaning of life

If you are a Muslim
you could try being a Sufi
speaking of greater truths
in between celebrations of movement

THE SANITY PATROL HANDBOOK

You could consider being a Gnostic
digging deeper into the mystical ramifications
of that which Jesus taught

Like it or not
the sin of practicing magick
is less of a sin
when dressed in different religious garb
Yet the source of the power is the same
a mystery that has many names
My tools come from the earth
My rites emulate the flow of nature
My artistry relies upon words and deeds
My beliefs recognize the dark, the light
and the twilight in between

Put a spin on sin
and turn it into a blessing
Then we can all be sinless
and spiritually sublime
in our own inimitable ways
Sin is a concept of the west
more useful in politics
than in a spiritual path

THE SANITY PATROL HANDBOOK

A POET PATROLLER SAYS:
Beware of eating apples
You will twin the original sin
We may all be siblings under the skin
but when it comes to the yang and the yin
and the heart and soul from within
sometimes revealed by a dumb grin
or a swift kick in the shin
when the action is grim
we want to begin
an original sin
The gin won't shut out the din
as your skin feels the pin
that has a prick
You thrust forth a chin
to conduct an original sin
by means of spin
as you rationalize
even when the argument is thin

Integrity will help you win
over the desire for original sin
For the sin is not original
It's a twin from without of that within
Look in the bin
and ask yourself
what came before the apple core?

IV. SELF MANAGEMENT

PAIRBONDING PATROLLERS

When two Patrollers come together
a bond is created
separate from the two Patrollers
The bond has a life of its own
as it secures the symmetrical warp and corresponding weave
that fabricates the relationship
The thicks and thinnesses that warp and weave
condition and recondition the bond
invoking responses from the two Patrollers

Can the bond between two Patrollers
be as healthy as each individual Patroller?
Maybe
Maybe not

Healthy bonds are described in verbs and adverbs
Adjectives and nouns describe a relationship
better served by fantasy
that makes for great stories and painful experiences
However
they sometimes serve as warm-ups for the aerobics of love

Transference is deadly
It occurs when
one Patroller misunderstands the qualities
of the intimacy shared

Projections of how another
could potentially fulfill the role
of a long lost relationship, especially a parent
turn reality into spectacle
The pressure on the other Patroller inpires actions of
     pushing far far away or
     indulging in countertransference
If healthily pushed away
the pursuing Patroller has the opportunity to figure out:
     What's missing in this picture?

However
if the Patroller being pursued pops into countertransference
the dualing projections create a diseased fog
so that the connection eats away
at both Patrollers personal perceptions
until soap operas and other high drama prevail

Transference demands expectation satisfaction
resulting in both patrollers revoking membership
Why?

Because what was assumed to be a healthy love relationship
is rooted in an inadequate child/parent connection
as opposed to the desire to orgasmitize, synchronize
and eat over-sized portions of chocolate and nuts
Symbiosis (co-dependence to the addictive)
dements the integrity of Patrollers
Bent backgrounds that break boundaries
confuse identity and dress up
like reassurance in drag
but are really the empty pockets
of slickly promoted promises and potential

Pairbonding Patrollers puzzle together
their plans of life in the privacy of their own intimacy
Problems that are personal are plowed with scythes
cutting at a personal past
In the present, passivity is replaced
by an assertive tentacle reaching out
for connection and understanding
Patrollers celebrate imperfection and differences
in the same breath they celebrate love

Plow on, Patrollers, plow on

THE SANITY PATROL HANDBOOK

THE DANCE OF URK, POO, EEK, UGH & AHHA

Every now and then
a Patroller gets
      overloaded
      overstimulated
      overindulgent
in its desire to provoke awakening in itself and others

The band at the base of the medulla vibrates
with visions of purring
Teeth grind
Cheeks well exercised seek exorcism
Blessed be the Kundalini that jolts the spine
Libido seeks Eros or Agape
Tension as nourishment interfaces with anxiety
Anxiety produces inertia
invoking a nervous lethargy

No sighs or depth of breath
A twitch becomes an itch which
alone acts as an outlet
Inlets overflow attempting to out run ecstasy
thus resulting in URK

URK dons many disguises
URK wears wings and abstract ones attention
URK wears lead boots and dull ones demonstrations
URK wears tight jeans and stimulate ones irritations
URK doesn't dance
URK moves without direction
    without discretion
    without dimension
Each step taken is without grace
marking the spots touched
like footprints in slow-freezing mud
URK is the sound stones make
when they are growing
URK is URK and knows not what this means

URK refracts into POO
POO skips a step up up up the stair
and stumbles down four more sore
POO drops
POO droops
POO dupes
Pout POO pout
POO forgets how to rock in the rhythmic rue
POO ponders POO

wandering the world in search of itself
Poo, says POO

POO distracts into EEK
EEK is an aimless arrow shot everywhere at once
embedding itself into anything and anyone that will react
EEK is not bleak
merely in search of the leak
to peak at where URK and POO came from
But EEK cannot concentrate longer than moments
EEK seeks something to hold onto
in order to fling it away

Once flung, EEK lapses into UGH
UGH's favorite food is grey
UGH's favorite flower is grey
UGH speaks grey
hears grey
and groans
The grey is bland
The bland is dull
The dull is safe and unchanging
No variation please

THE SANITY PATROL
HANDBOOK

The grey is bland
The bland is dull
The dull is safe and unchanging
Sameness abounds and astounds nothing

Can there be hope?
Does there exist a fan strong enough to manifest distinction?
Boredom
No, no, cries UGH
This cannot be
Not boredom!
Please!
Too late
The meticulous tedium breaker is ignited
and the fan fires up revolution
UGH is evoluted
and taken to the Transitory Grounds
The Transitory Grounds hold everything
        from maybes
        to in betweens
        to the hold it -- let me see
Some never leave the Transitory Grounds
They roll around in potential
but never actually accomplish anything

Escape can be easy
First one bows to honor URK, POO, EEK and UGH
Next, one learns to dance with mutable movement
in order to cry
        to laugh
        to shrug
        to let go
        to grieve
        and to leave
because URK, POO, EEK and UGH are dead
Long live the dead

The grave sights available
for URK, POO, EEK and UGH
lie in the Acceptance Cemetery
the bodies are viewed
        reviewed
        and viewed again
        until they are seen
Once accepted
they are ready for the worms

Dig deep
Burial takes effort

THE SANITY PATROL HANDBOOK

Effort stimulates transformation and transition
The clouds that hung heavy and perpetuated gloom
burst into rain and wash away tears of fears, rage, hurt and pain
The band of the medulla is relieved, released and goes home

New energy lets heath emerge
The funnel of awareness expands to allow a greater flow
Adrenals at work awaken

AH HA takes center stage
        smiles
        titters
        laughs
        guffaws
disintegrating over this
and too much that
Vibrations are rhythmic
and purr as AH HA arises rested and relaxed

Congratulations, Patroller
you made it through the dance again
Pathology is renewed

THE BOZO PILL

Sometimes Patrollers wish to quit – temporarily

They seek the comfort of narcissism
    the bliss of blindness
    the ease of denial
    the freedom of insanity

What to do what to do take a pill
A bozo pill
Down it and drown in the desire not to care
Swallow it to swing swirl and sing out the joys of density
in the dense city of humanity awaiting
    with arms like those of the statue of Venus
    with warmth like that of fireflies
    with the love like that of cannibals

"You're safe as long as you refuse progress disown growth renounce awareness"
the bozo gods smirk
"Close your eyes and take short shallow breaths
Deplete your ego and blend blend blend
    with the unacknowledged ambiguity of your surroundings
    with the unanswerable ambivalence of your environment
Careful

You wouldn't want to awaken would you?
In the mouth out the nose
If you breathe wrong you might make embarrassing and uncivilized sounds
like snorting burping and belching
Not a good thing
Breathe too deep and you just might fart
And we all know how we feel about those full of hot stinky air
who simply can't contain themselves
So breathe breathe breathe with self-consciousness
as though everyone were watching you
Good

"Imagine the world revolves around you
You establish all moralities
You decide what is good and what is bad
Nothing you do or feel is wrong
You are God in your wisdom – compassion if you like
You are the Goddess in your love of life – your own of course
All that is you is correct
Go ahead change the rules
Foolish consistency is a ghostly hobgoblin
and not worthy of your attention
Reduce your awareness of others
They may be harmful to your health
Your ignorance is everyone's ignorance
Your naiveté is everyone's naiveté

THE SANITY PATROL HANDBOOK

Your inadequacy is everyone's inadequacy
Information you do not possess does not exist
If you can't figure it out no one can

"Your learning comes from those you allow to be a temporary authority
Careful
you may lose respect for their authority and have to decide
whether or not their information is still valid
You are the one and only thing in the universe that matters
If you didn't feel that way you would have never allowed yourself
    to be born
    to incarnate
    from incarcerated energy to matter
Soul? If you like
The collective unconscious gives you permission to have connection
while remaining alienated superior and spiteful
of those with whom you are forced to share an existence
Therefore
the content that is you is actually all everything and everybody Om"

We are one
You are one
We are you
You the one who knows we are one
The one who knows we
The one who knows

One knows
One nose
One I
Two eyes
Two eyes one nose
I? Knows?
I knows one nose
I knows two eyes
Eyes nose
Damn I –
the words
The words made me do it
I'm not crazy
I know one nose two eyes
I –
the numbers
The numbers made me do it
I'm not crazy
There is one word too many
There are one two many words
Is there an Arithmetic Linguist in the house?

So that's it
The bozo pill is wearing off
Time for reintegration
Truly a pain in the assets of sanity

THE SANITY PATROL HANDBOOK

V. THE FIVE SOCIETIES OF THE SANITY PATROL

SANITY PATROL SUBSOCIETIES

Most Patrollers belong to one or more subsocieties
because they are diversified in their interests
Perusing the qualifications for each subsociety
helps Patrollers better understand their divergences
let alone themselves
In this way
Patrollers can better support one another
especially when retaining the services of a fellow Patroller

> to enhance well being
> to establish a group entity
> to add creative spice
> to learn a new something or
> to seek spiritual enlightenment

Generally speaking, the subsocieties as they stand at this time are:

PERSONAL CAREGIVERS OF POSITIVE CONCERN
include psychologists, therapists, nurses, doctors, lawyers,
alternative healers, and other servicers of humans who are
needful

ASSOCIATED BUSINESS & COMMUNITY DEVELOPERS (ABCD)

lead groups of humans for purposes of profit, advocacy, the support of a special interest or other groupings

ARTSY SMARTSY SOCIETY OF UNCOOPERATIVES (ASSU)

support those creatively compelled to produce works of art within all venues available or those yet to arrive

ESSENTIAL EDUCATORS OF THE ELEMENTS OF EXISTENCE (EEEE)

brings together those in the service helping others learn to think by providing strategies in assembling and analyzing information

DUALISTIC ORDER OF DEMONSTRATIVE ORACLES (DODO)

is split into two disputing factions who observe past and present and then may or may not use additional tools to predict the future

PERSONAL CAREGIVERS OF POSITIVE CONCERN (PCPC)

Are you compelled, compulsed or committed to helping others?
Maybe it's your desire or maybe it's demanded of you
this servicing for those who cannot do it for themselves?
If you are inspired to respond
welcome to the Personal Caregivers of Positive Concern or PCPC
You are either a Delegated Caregiver or a Caregiving Pro
Neither group is required to be politically correct
even though they tend towards that orientation
Why?
Because Caregivers see through the eyes of others
with empathetic awareness
and sympathetic understanding
Yes
You care
You are concerned
You want to help
You possess special skills and abilities to assist
or positioning resembling same

and offer your services willingly or unwillingly
Lucky you

Some Patrollers suggest
most caregivers are crazy
becoming caregivers as a way of caring for themselves
Maybe this is so and maybe it's not
Craziness does not necessarily exclude sanity
or impair a caregiver's ability to help the needful
Yes, even the well trained wacky
can be capable of performing this work
except for sometimes
Why?
Caregivers often search for answers
to the same questions asked by the needful
including existential unanswerables
that demand more acceptance than content
and what's more -- they know it

Caregiving relates to anything
        from the therapeutic to the bureaucratic
        from the legal to the redemptive
Caregivers help those who have issues
that get in the way of good living
sometimes in the guise of stupidity
but more often the result of ignorance
or crappy early conditioning

DELEGATED CARGIVERS

are responsible for
      a newborn baby
      an aging or dying family member
      a mentally ill sibling or parent
      a seriously ailing autonomous friend
      or some facsimile thereof
It may be a spiritual community or government agency doing the caregiving
due to a lack of family willing, able or existing
Financial factors play a vital role
in how and from whom a needy person receives care
Sacrifices of sorts can be demanded of Delegated Caregivers
who must learn to accept their new priorities
as part of caring for the needful
This can cause tremendous stress
in maintaining membership as a Patroller
Charity is a good and necessary act
but only the self-full can afford to be selfless

A Delegated Caregiver is not required to relish the fact
they are responsible for a needy person
Nor do they have to perfectly attend
to all of the needs therein
Each situation is unique and brings up its own old baggage

even when what's packed isn't enough to sustain a gnat
and you feel like you're taking a trip to nowhere
Fortunately, mistakes, missteps and mishaps
cause only temporary revocation of membership
if the Delegated Caregiver does the work necessary
to bring themselves back into compliance
Carry on, Delegated Caregiver
but don't carry on too much
or you will have to check yourself in somewhere

CAREGIVING PROS

have skill sets and talent to do what they do
They also have credentials to prove it
Whether knowledge comes from an academic institution or specified training
their experience shapes their innate abilities and all they have studied
Caregiving Pros are paid to help others
or at least that's one of their goals
Those who perform caregiving in the name of a spiritual path
rely upon that spiritual institution
to provide sustenance and basic needs
which is comparable to getting paid
at least most of the time
Caregiving Pros cannot haphazardly or freely give away
their hard-earned knowledge or cultivated efforts
Why?
Such acts of sublimating all sense of Self is insane

The Sanity Patrol Handbook

and leaves no room for integrity or individuation
Some Caregiving Pros walk that fine line between
doing their jobs and being a mentsh
because a little extra support just might make
all the difference in the world
to someone in need

However
        if compassion turns to meddling
        if empathy becomes all-consuming or
        if other behaviors challenge one's ability to maintain
                a separate identify from those in need
a Caregiving Pro must re-evaluate their boundary setting abilities
if they wish to maintain membership in the Sanity Patrol

Confucius say, "Healers are dealers of hope."
Both Delegated Caregivers and Caregiving Pros know this
and remind one another regularly to keep them on track
helping each other avoid burn out
or becoming too cynical to help anyone else
Sadly for the members of the Personal Caregivers of Positive Concern
the best result they can anticipate
is being left behind
as the object of their care embraces their own life or death

THE SANITY PATROL HANDBOOK

ASSOCIATED BUSINESS & COMMUNITY DEVELOPERS (ABCD)

The ABCD includes those Patrollers who lead groups of humans
who share a common cause, special interest or profit motive
These Patrollers are known as Alphas
There are three subsocieties of Alphas

COM DEVS are committed to various voluntary causes or special interest groups
who bring together those who share ideas or needs
and seek to develop their communal orientation

BIZ BAKERS seek alliances or underwriting
to create, establish and grow business concerns
that provide sustenance along with extras

RIGHTEOUS GOVERNORS are paid to aid
by means of a government agency
whether it be local, county, state, federal or international
often receiving negative press as bureaucrats or politicians

Any society or community in which we live
relies on the ABCD to function
Yes
Alphas run the world
They each possess a bounty of leadership skills
giving the groupings they lead confidence and trust
that their individual needs will be met.

You know you're an Alpha if:

YOU HAVE A BIG MOUTH
When in a group
whether it be a deliberate clumping
or an arbitrary collective
yours is a voice that is heard
Like a magnet you attract
the focus of the group
except for those few contraries
who are not attracted to anyone or anything anyway
When challenged by conflict within a grouping
you find that larger perspective
that makes moot the disagreement
allowing opposing opinions to peacefully co-exist
by embracing rather that resolving ambiguity
and making you look good

YOU'RE BOSSY AND EVERYONE KNOWS IT

You are perceived as an important contributor
or maybe an ultimate authority
who can articulate and assimilate ideas of others
when planning actions to be taken
or a philosophy to embrace
Even when you don't know the correct answer
you respond in a way
that satisfies the inquirer
demonstrating the importance of your opinion

YOU SEE PAST THE END OF YOUR OWN NEEDS

You have the vision to see past details
and predict a final outcome
yet are practical enough to also figure out
how to get from here to there
convincing the individuals of the group
with your contagious confidence
that the actions you plan will work
You let the itching sensation of discontent drive you
to greater visionary tasks you endeavor to actualize
accepting the loneliness of your often precarious role

YOU GET OTHER PEOPLE TO DO STUFF

You know you can't do it all by yourself
so you recruit those who can do some of it
They have their own skills and knowledge
and want to use them to bring forth your vision
You honor their expertise
and trust they will fulfill their duties
with just a little supervision
as they seek out your praise and acceptance

YOU'RE GOOD

You have the wisdom to take the high road
when given the option
You are persistent and have the endurance
to see a process through to completion
because the end will justify the effort
You recognize failure when you see it
take it in stride and move on
assuming mistakes are part of the process
of building an empire with a secure foundation
You take responsibility when failure happens
without taking it personally
or letting it put a damper on taking new risks

THE SANITY PATROL HANDBOOK

YOU POLITIC POSITIONING AND POWER

Your recruits trust your ability to lead them
through the bad times as well as the good
recognizing your integrity and trustworthiness
You may not like the manipulations and machinations of politics
but you understand what it means to be political
and take advantage of opportunities for better positioning
that enhances your power to do what comes next

Alphas may not love the details of strategic planning
but they know they must embrace them anyway
learning the elements that outline and integrate vital information
so that when Alphas speak they know what they're talking about

Alphas who lead only by means of charisma and platitudes
such as cult leaders, religious leaders and politicians
do not usually maintain Sanity Patrol membership
even if they think they are qualified
The real Patrollers know this and treat them accordingly

THE SANITY PATROL HANDBOOK

ESSENTIAL EDUCATORS OF THE ELEMENTS OF EXISTENCE (EEEE)

Patrollers who are members of EEEE
largely teach children, teenagers and young adults
looking to find a place for themselves in the world
because Educators are always on the lookout for young Sanity Patrol recruits
who could just as easily become anti-patroller if misdirected
Other Educators teach adults seeking new inspiration
or possibly the regeneration of cellular activity in their brains
that perpetuates curiosity and a need to know
Despite countless tests and studies
no one can easily articulate
what makes a masterful educator

General characteristics of effective Educators include

YOU ACCOMODATE FOR VARIATIONS

Educators design their curricular activities
to accommodate different learning strategies
Some students respond more to – look at that over there
Others respond to – take a whiff and tell me what stinks
or – read this book and you'll get it, honest
Some prefer text only
others want the graphics

Some like the dramas of pressure
while others prefer untimed tests or self-pacing methods
and so on ad infinitum or bite 'em
Some Educators use daily rituals
to tie the teaching points together into a line
giving an ongoing rhythm to the learning song
that encourages students to go along
Whatever the strategy
organization and precision are demanded
with dashes of flexibility and goofiness

YOU ACTUALLY KNOW SOMETHING

Educators have to know what they're teaching about duh
and be able to answer peripheral and tangential questions
when on a roll in an area of non-expertise
An Educator may realize that they don't have a clue
and direct students to someone or something who does
Educators know they can't know it all
but they can put on a good show of knowing
Their openness to learning can be infectious
their tenacious curiosity contagious
so that learning becomes a chronic disease
Enthusiasm for learning makes for an effective Educator
This extends to both the subject matter and the students
and the belief that the two are compatible
and on the verge of merging

Educators have a capacity for empathy and compassion
that reaches out and into their students' beings
so they can better assess
a student's unique abilities, difficulties and obstacles
The social-economic needs of students
will demand an Educator's attention like it or not
Educators often disagree amongst themselves
on the fine points of dealing with this disparity
Therefore
labels, categorization, accusations and blame are dumb
simplistic ways of pretending to solve complex problems

YOU KNOW COMMUNICATION WORKS BOTH WAYS

Two-way communication encourages curiosity
or so most Educators believe
Charisma is a plus when communicating with a class
turning enthusiasm into inspiration into results
However
not all Educators are particularly charismatic
Some rely on one-to-one communication
to motivate their students into action
When an Educator is honest about how they feel
whether it be joyous, frustrated or enraged
responsibility is transferred directly to the student
in how that student chooses to act
And who knows?

THE SANITY PATROL HANDBOOK

Maybe the student will learn and practice
self observation and evaluation
A sense of humor can diffuse bombs of frustration
when struggling with new ideas
        or insinuating information
        or bypassing resistence

Education is not measurable
Sure, Educators comply with all the test-taking
but they recognize the results do not necessarily reflect
the knowledge, awareness and potential of students
or even of fellow educators

However
Educators do their utmost best
to perform their jobs to the satisfaction of all
establishing as healthy a relationship as can be had
with parents and other integral participants in a student's life
as part of the educational process
Why?
Because that's what they've learned to do
and that's what works

DUALIZED ORDER OF DEMONSTRATIVE ORACLES (DODO)

The Dualized Order of Demonstrative Oracles or DODO
consists of two very separate disparate groups
Their major disagreements are largely due
to differences in how they perceive time and space

INSTANT LOGICIANS embrace linear time
They reflect on the past
live in the moment
and use their knowledge to try and predict a logical future
They believe magic is merely a manipulation of the mind
They are pragmatic in their approach
attributing the notion of intuition
to analyzing and assimilating data very quickly
and coming up with a logical conclusion
Instant Logicians want to believe
that if common sense were common
everyone would be Instant Logicians
The road to ultimate conclusions
may be difficult to back track
but can ultimately and eventually be done

The mysteries of the universe are only mysteries
because they haven't been figured out yet
Although it took a while to convince them
many Instant Logicians have finally incorporated
notions of quantum mechanics
although they prefer committing to the idea
that true objectivity really does exist
They have learned to accept that subjectivity colors reality
so that when the tints and hues of subjectivity are aligned
with an individual or group
mapping the road of logical analysis becomes obvious
Therefore
synchronizing subjectivity fuels the movement towards
logical conclusions that resemble oracles
but were derived using the information available
The illusions of magic seem so very real
but always have a logical explanation
or so the Instant Logicians believe

INTUITION MASTERS embrace the notion
that time and space are the result of consensus reality
and don't necessarily exist outside human perception
They believe magick can result from ritual
or the use of symbolic systems
or other developing possibilities
No rational explanations can articulate
how awakening and enlightenment arises

THE SANITY PATROL
HANDBOOK

When connections are made, meaning surfaces
inspiring a new sense of awareness
The meaning may not easily be articulated
but is often sensed by every cell in the body
Intuitive Masters insist that divining the future
as oracles are inclined to do
is less about predicting the future
and more about giving meaning to what may possibly happen
Those who value sessions with professional Intuitive Masters
often leave with something other than what they expected
with or without specifics to report to others
and unconcerned about articulating their experience
because the experience itself was meaningful

The Instant Logicians and Intuitive Masters
are at odds more than not
scoffing at the other's efforts
Yet a third group emerges – members of both groups
even if they don't admit it shhhh
The fact that Patrollers can so vehemently disagree
does not lessen the strength of the Sanity Patrol
Facts may be consistent
Observations not so much
but truth is a mutable monster
that strikes the heart – not the mind

THE ARTSY SMARTSY SOCIETY OF UNCOOPERATIVES (ASSU)

Do you qualify to be a member of ASSU and call yourself an ASSette?
Consider
Are you compelled to put forth your ideas, perceptions and visions
through a medium of expression such as
music, visual art, movement, film or the written word?
Do you cultivate your skills to enhance those expressions?
Are your expressions a means of communicating something to others?

Are you paradoxical in that:

Creativity energizes you but
you quietly think through the expression
that creative energy takes

You are unusually bright but
you are also incredibly naive
and more gullible than you'll admit

You love to play and break the rules but
you take your creative expression seriously
only breaking the rules after you've learned them

You have an imagination that continually expands but
you have a solid awareness of reality mostly
and your feet touch the ground

Creative expression produces a kind of grandiose high but
you are humbled by a project's completion
and honored by the result

You may have many projects percolating
at different stages of development but
you have completed one or more somethings

You are passionate about your work but
you maintain objectivity in assessing it
and have learned how to take in critique

You experience the pain and frustration of creativity but
you know intimately its joy
satisfaction and release

An ASSette doesn't dabble or
pine for time to create or
need to make a piece of work perfect or
fear what others may think

THE SANITY PATROL HANDBOOK

No
The ASSette is compelled to create
more often pines for normalcy and
needs to see a piece of work finished
When opportunities for show are not easily available
ASSettes recognize luck and timing are not on their side
and create their own opportunities to present their work
ASSettes know that success comes and goes
learning to embrace those sacred moments when
they connect with an audience
so that something larger and greater than themselves
gives their lives and those of their audience meaning and value

However
pursuing these avenues while maintaining membership in the Sanity Patrol
can be challenging and sometimes seemingly close to impossible
The creative madness that ensues
is not pretty to those who experience it
This is why all artsy Patrollers are required to join ASSU
and perhaps serve on a subsociety or two

Yes
You can get help managing the madness of your unique being
ASSettes are often in need of special reminders
that struggling with creative madness does not preclude Patrol membership

THE SANITY PATROL HANDBOOK

Your madness as an ASSette results from this compulsion to create
Perhaps there was a time you could hang out with artsy anti-patrollers
but now you pursue authentic success
Their pretentiousness provokes rolling eyes and annoyance
because they don't back up their ideas with actual work

Besides
the current market for expressions of creativity excludes
self-indulgence and dramatic demonstrations
except for sometimes

Each of you ASSettes must design a strategic plan
that will remind you of who and how you are
The needs of the creative process are ever so personal
You may find yourself regularly reaching out for validation
that serves both your need to impact an audience
and your need for help delineating where your identity ends
and where your work begins

ASSettes know that presentation requires collaboration
designing effective madness management strategies
is also a collaborative process
despite the fact that on the path of innovation
each ASSette walks
alone

THE SANITY PATROL HANDBOOK

By serving on the ASSU
you will learn how to recognize a fellow ASSette
who needs validation
and know how to offer them support
according to their individual strategic plan
 Other Patrollers may not see the point
but they are trained to honor and respect it
even though they may not understand it
Careful, ASSettes
Sometimes they forget their training

The ASSU applauds your success
and reminds you that you have been successful
when failure or struggle returns
which it often does since success is cyclic
unless you have crossed over into stardom
You few who reach humungous commercial success
may find yourselves confused by your audiences
They may be more interested in you
than in your work
What's private becomes media fodder
What's personal becomes universal
Careful
Self-imposed isolation resulting from public recognition
can seduce a Patroller into revoking their membership
The ASSU will share your joy of success

THE SANITY PATROL HANDBOOK

during those fleeting moments when
your satisfied audience grows and expands
Acknowledgement may be transitory
but those special moments of direct or indirect recognition
nurture your creative development for a long time
and protect your Sanity Patrol membership

The ASSU does not include those who use creativity
as a means of self-actualization
The ASSU may be tempted to include them
but wannabees are a serious pain in the ASSU
and are asked to continue creating
but remove themselves from the ASSU
All ASSettes, in collaboration with the ASSU
are required to make distinctions and discriminate
the desirous from the compulsed
as part of the personal madness management program
so they know better on whom to rely
for validation and support

Some ASSettes must serve on a subsociety of the ASSU
that focuses on specific mediums, venues or genres
Some subsocieties focus on multi-discipline models
        audience development
        or other issue-oriented concerns of the ASSU
The support you receive by serving a subsociety

reinforces your strategic plan
deepens your relationship with your art
and reduces the risk of membership revocation
Those ASSettes who do not serve on a subsociety or three
may find they push the envelope that holds their membership card
If the envelope should open the membership card could be lost
amidst the other papers that insulate the world
replacement membership cards are available
but demand dramatic demonstrations to prove worthiness

Another issue for many ASSettes
is that of sustenance
Creativity may feed the soul
but at a certain point
you will wish this creative fodder to become literally edible
Multi-tasking is often mandatory
The day job may surprise you
in how it keeps you connected to your audience
So
do not despair at a dualistic existence
and repeat 50 times daily:
"I am an ASSette and a member of the subsociety of [fill in the blank]
and maintain full membership
in the Sanity Patrol"
You are the real thing, you ASSette you

so please – carry on

THE SANITY PATROL HANDBOOK

VI. FUTURE PUBLICATIONS OF THE SANITY PATROL PRESS

For ease of selection, future publications of The Sanity Patrol Press are listed by subsociety:

THE PERSONAL CAREGIVERS OF POSITIVE CONCERN

PSYCH BYTES, succinctly articulates the basics of psychology
  STRATEGIES OF SANITY, depicts various therapeutic orientations
CALLING PEOPLE NAMES, serves as an unusual and visceral diagnostic guide
  INTERVENTIONS AHOY, explores many popular therapies
  MANAGING MADNESS, guides the depressed through healthy self-help
  MEDICATE, MEDICATE, DANCE TO THE MUSIC, looks at the many medications used for mental illness

ASSOCIATED BUSINESS & COMMUNITY DEVELOPERS

  THE MEDIA MADE ME DO IT, examines the effects of media on culture, community and individuals
  WE CAN DO THIS, looks at organizational development and leadership

ARTSY SMARTSY SOCIETY OF UNCOOPERATIVES

  SANITY PATROL PARABLES, compiles short stories for all occasions
THEATER OF THE MIND, provides games and scripting for everyday life
  WRITE ON, SANITY PATROL, offers writing exercises for both technical development and self-exploration
THE Z TECHNIQUE OF CRITIQUE, explores an author-focused stategy for assessing new works

ESSENTIAL EDUCATORS OF THE ELEMENTS OF EXISTENCE
THE SANITY PATROL DOES DIVORCE, a common sense guide to dissolution litigation
I SAY, YOU SAY, WE SAY, THEY SAY identifies the elements of communication

DUALISTIC ORDER OF DEMONSTRATIVE ORACLES
*TAROT POETRY, uses the Tarot as a model for sanity-producing poetry
SANITY MAINTENANCE RITUALS, demonstrates magic and magick tools used to reinforce sanity

*to be published by 2005

The Sanity Patrol Press anticipates producing games designed to alter attitudes, modify behaviors and provoke sanity in those who play them.

To order a membership pin that says: "I am a member of the Sanity Patrol" go to The Sanity Patrol Press' website: http://www.thesanitypatrol.com

The Sanity Patrol Players offer 10 minute, 30 minute and 90 minute multi-media presentations that use material from this *Handbook*. Check http://www.thesanitypatrol.com for more information.

REPRIEVE

The Sanity Patrol is out to get you
You, the nitchless, the warp in the weave the shuttle entwines to fabricate reality
You, the unfitable, proud of your distinction, individuated and mystically correct
You, the unique, providing an eye for an eye in the needle that embroiders
      the appliqué that is you making your mark
You, the choreographer, dancing with the angels on the head of a pin
The Sanity Patrol has come
      to nourish
      to flourish
      to relish
      in your Being
      to celebrate
      to invigorate
      to internally investigate
      the more
      the better
      the best
That is yours
      ours
      amen
      a women
      a singular
      a plural
You
The Sanity Patrol is out to get you

SONG OF THE SANITY PATROL

The Sanity Patrol is out to get you
Are you a Patroller too
The Sanity Patrol is out to get you
What you think you're gonna do

If you find peace of mind in common sense
The Sanity Patrol wants you
If you have emotional intelligence
The Sanity Patrol wants you
If you like to argue but take no offense
The Sanity Patrol wants you
If you don't like everyone but have tolerance
The Sanity Patrol wants you

The Sanity Patrol is out to get you
There's no place for you to hide
The Sanity Patrol is out to get you
Get a Handbook and look inside

Z. Sharon Glantz is co-author of Stages of Ages: Rechilding and Regression with Elaine Childs-Gowell, Ph.D. She writes and produces plays, her greatest successes providing live theater on issues such as diversity, sexual harassment, HIV/AIDS and aging as part of training programs for corporations, educational institutions and government agencies. Other scriptwriting credits include an orientation video for the State of Washington Apprentice in the Trades Program, a laser show for the educational system in Singapore on that country's history and a multi-media presentation using a live actor and video to teach high school students about the holocaust. She has served as program director on the board of the Pacific Northwest Writers Association and was co-founder of the Northwest Playwrights Guild. Her novel, *The Masterpack*, a comedic thriller about a pack of dogs and their people who walk a Seattle park illegally without leashes, will be published in 2004. She uses her website, http://www.thesanitypatrol.com, to promote her work as well as to experiment with various forms of hyperfiction.

For more information on the books available from The Sanity Patrol Press or presentations offered by The Sanity Patrol Players, visit http://www.thesanitypatrol.com